PHOSPHORESCENT INTELLIGENCE

THE GLOW THAT STAYS:
REIMAGINING LEADERSHIP FROM
BURNOUT TO BELONGING, AND
CULTURE TO SUSTAINABLE GROWTH

LESLEY VALLANCE

First published by Busybird Publishing 2025

Copyright © 2025 Lesley Vallance

ISBN
Print: 978-1-923501-32-4

This work is copyright. Apart from any use permitted under the
Copyright Act 1968, no part of this publication may be reproduced,
stored in a retrieval system or transmitted in any form or by any means,
electronic, mechanical, photocopying, recording or otherwise,
without the prior written permission of Lesley Vallance.

The information in this book is based on the author's experiences and opinions. The author and publisher disclaim responsibility for any adverse consequences that may result from use of the information contained herein. Permission to use any external content has been sought by the author. Any breaches will be rectified in further editions of the book.

Cover Image: Lesley Vallance

Cover design: Lesley Vallance

Layout and typesetting: Busybird Publishing

Busybird Publishing
2/118 Para Road
Montmorency, Victoria
Australia 3094
www.busybird.com.au

Overview

*P*hosphorescent Intelligence explores how a sustained, adaptive, and holistic form of intelligence can transform workplace culture, leadership, and business growth. In a world fatigued by burnout and performative leadership, this book offers a new way forward – where wellbeing is not an afterthought, but an essential foundation.

Drawing from lived experience, organisational change, and human-centred leadership, this work introduces a different kind of intelligence. One that lingers, illuminates, and elevates. One that centres people, purpose, and presence.

This is not just a methodology. It is a movement. It is not about shining for attention.

It is about glowing with intention.

CONTENTS

Preface: A Life That Glows	1
Foreword	3
From Flash to Glow	5
The Cultural Impact	10
Leadership By Luminescence	16
Person-Centric Business Models	24
The Business Model of The Future	33
Beyond Survival: The Economics of Thriving	34
The Growth Mindset	40
Tools And Frameworks for Implementation	47
Real Stories, Real Fire	54
The Workplaces of Tomorrow	61
Epilogue: The Manifesto Of the Glowing Ones	69
References	83

Preface: A Life That Glows

This isn't just a book. It is my soul stitched into pages. A quiet revolution written with fire.

I was never meant to fit the mould. As a neurodivergent child with dyslexia, I spent years in classrooms where my curiosity was misunderstood, and my intuition dismissed. But even then, I felt something – the flicker. The glow. A deep knowledge that my difference wasn't a flaw. It was fuel.

For too long, we have defined intelligence in narrow and rigid ways. And being measured by standards never built for you brings a specific kind of grief. But that grief also creates grit. And that grit becomes fire. And compassion. And vision. That is where this story begins.

In 2015, I moved from Scotland to Australia with a suitcase and a fierce devotion to change.

By 2020, I had founded Holistic Growth Solutions. Not with a detailed roadmap, but with a deep belief that workplaces could be different – more human, more sustainable, more aware.

The Facilities Management industry was my entry point. I loved it. I still do. But I saw cracks in its foundation – cracks that were not limited to one sector. These are systemic. And I could no longer look away.

In 2023, I co-founded a demolition company, and that experience widened my view again.

It revealed just how much is missing in the construction space, especially when it comes to people and care. It deepened my resolve.

This book was born from that resolve. It is not a theory. It is lived experience. It is not a concept. It is conviction.

It is not about fitting in. It is about illuminating what was there all along.

Phosphorescent intelligence is the kind of intelligence I have lived, led, fought for, and embedded into every organisation I have supported. It is not about visibility. It is about impact. It is not loud. It lingers.

And so do we – the difference-makers, the ones who carry quiet conviction, the ones who refuse to dim.

This is for the leader who is tired of pretending.

For the neurodivergent child still waiting to be heard. For every team that deserves more than survival.

This is the book I needed when I began. And now, it is yours.

Let it glow.

Foreword

In a time of profound transformation across industries globally, this book emerges as both a guide and a grounding force. While it was born out of real-world application in Facilities Management, the ideas and frameworks presented here extend well beyond one sector. From hospitals to classrooms, startups to NGOs, the concept of phosphorescent intelligence offers a regenerative lens to reimagine leadership, wellbeing, and performance.

From Flash to Glow: Understanding Phosphorescent Intelligence

Most of us were raised to chase the flash.

Be the brightest. Be the loudest. Arrive first. Say the cleverest thing in the room. Make your mark. Win the award. Hit the target.

And I've done all of that. I've stood on the podium, spoken on the stage, worn the heels that hurt just enough to say, 'I mean business'. But here's what no one told us: flash fades.

Phosphorescent intelligence is different.

It doesn't burn out. It doesn't demand constant attention. It glows – quietly, powerfully, and sustainably. Long after the room empties. Long after the spotlight moves. It is in this glow where real, lasting transformation lives. And that's what makes the difference – not just in people, but in culture and leadership.

Flash vs Glow (And Why Glow Matters)

Flash is the quarterly win that's forgotten six months later. Glow is the leader whose impact is still felt five years on.

Flash is loud. Glow listens.

Flash says, 'Look at me.' Glow says, 'I see you.' The world of work has long rewarded flash. But the future? It belongs to the glow.

Different Generations, Different Lens

In every workplace I've worked in – especially in Facilities Management – there's been a beautiful blend of generations, each bringing their own rhythms and expectations. So how does phosphorescent intelligence land across these age groups?

Baby Boomers (Born 1946-1964)

Raised on loyalty, long hours, and resilience, Boomers sometimes see this kind of intelligence as too soft – until they connect it with legacy. Glow, for them, becomes the wisdom and culture they leave behind.

'I've built this business over 30 years. The glow is what ensures it still stands 30 more.'

Generation X (Born 1965-1980)

Independent, often understated, and masters of quiet competence, Gen X values the glow when it translates to credibility and efficiency. They're not chasing attention – they want impact that lasts.

'Don't waste my time. But if it helps the team grow, I'm in.'

Millennials (Born 1981-1996)

Purpose-driven, wellbeing-aware, and allergic to performance for performance's sake, Millennials speak fluent glow. They crave workplaces where authenticity is the norm and wellbeing isn't a box to tick.

'Can I bring my whole self to work? If not, I'll find somewhere I can.'

Generation Z (Born 1997-2012)

Bold, conscious, and unafraid to speak truth to power, Gen Z demands workplaces that are psychologically safe and ethically sound. Glow isn't aspirational for them – it's expected.

'We're not afraid to leave. Lead with heart or don't lead at all.'

The Principles of Phosphorescent Intelligence

Depth Over Dazzle

You don't have to be the loudest to be the most respected.

Sustainability Over Speed

Quick wins are just that – quick. Glowing cultures take time to build, but they last.

Presence Over Performance

Be with people, not above them. Connection matters more than output alone.

What It Looks Like

A seasoned site manager who mentors without ego.

A Gen Z office assistant who creates a lunchtime mental health check-in circle.

A Gen X team leader who starts every toolbox talk with, 'How are you really doing?'

This kind of intelligence doesn't fade when the lights go off. It's not about being seen. It's about being felt.

Why This Matters in Facilities Management (And Why I Stayed)

Facilities Management might not always get the attention, but it holds everything else up. It is the backbone of buildings, safety, and seamless operations.

Yes, it's long been a male-dominated, hard-Yaka kind of space. But I've never found more honesty or integrity anywhere else, and that's why I stayed. It's why I started Holistic Growth Solutions. It's why I walk onto job sites still feeling lit up by the possibilities. And it's why I believe this industry, more than most, is ready for a different kind of intelligence.

So whether you're a Boomer thinking about the legacy you'll leave, a Gen X leader building system, a Millennial driving cultural balance, or a Gen Z voice demanding better – this glow is for you.

It's time to stop chasing the flash.

It's time to create workplaces that glow through.

The Cultural Impact: Creating A Sustained Glow in The Workplace

What Happens When Culture Isn't Just Built, but Charged?

Most businesses talk about culture like it's something you install – like new software. But what if culture could do more than just operate? What if it could store light?
Glow in the dark?
Outlast the pressure?
Outlive the moment?

That is the vision of phosphorescent intelligence.

Not a corporate fad. Not another compliance module. Not something to laminate and stick in a break room.

But something human. Alive. Grounded.

Built for the long haul.

This kind of culture absorbs meaning in the quiet, learns in the background, and holds light until it's needed most.

It stays when everything else feels like it's slipping away.

From Fluorescent to Phosphorescent

Most workplace cultures still chase that fluorescent brightness – immediate, harsh, always on. The kind of culture that demands urgency, visibility, results.

But phosphorescent culture is different.

It stores energy. It absorbs care. It learns in the silence. It glows when the lights go off.

This is not performative wellness. This is emotional equity. This is safety that doesn't need signage to exist.

It's dignity – embedded.

A Real-Life Glow: The Cleaning Crew at 4 am

I've witnessed this kind of culture before sunrise.

During a site visit at 4 am, while most of the city slept, I watched a cleaner whisper good morning to the coffee machine. She wasn't being quirky. She was grounding herself. That coffee machine had become a ritual. That worksite – a kind of home.

That's phosphorescent culture.

Where silence is respected. Where routine is revered.

Where even the smallest roles hold space for pride.

Culture Is What Happens in the In-Between

It's not the town hall meeting. It's what happens the day after.

It's:

- the unsent email that avoids shame
- the mid-week check-in that becomes a lifeline
- the supervisor who remembers your name, your kid's name, and your shift start time
- the foreperson in demolition who asks, 'How are you holding up?' and actually waits for an answer.

It's the difference between tolerance and trust. Between compliance and care.

I've stood in rooms where the culture allowed me to stutter, then breathe, then rise. I've seen workers crack open and be held – not judged.

And I've watched teams rebuild after burnout – not through better metrics, but through better connection.

Why This Matters for Safety

In industries where risk is daily – where sharp tools, heavy machinery, working at heights, or long shifts are part of the job – safety culture can't rely on paperwork alone. It has to live in people.

Phosphorescent intelligence strengthens safety culture not by replacing systems, but by deepening the human connections that make those systems work.

When people feel psychologically safe, they speak up sooner. They report hazards, they question instructions that feel off, they check in on the person next to them. And when leaders glow – when they lead with presence, empathy, and consistency – safety becomes cultural, not conditional.

This glow-based approach creates environments where:

- team members are more likely to raise concerns early

- fatigue and burnout are seen as safety risks, not signs of weakness

- supervisors model calm, human first decision-making – especially under pressure

- safety protocols aren't resented, they're respected, because they protect people who feel valued.

In one demolition crew I worked with, the introduction of daily 'pulse checks' – just two minutes for each worker to voice how they were feeling before the shift – led to a noticeable drop in incidents. Not because people tried harder, but because they felt seen. They felt safe.

Safety culture thrives when emotional safety comes first.

Glowing Isn't Passive – It's an Act of Leadership

To build this kind of culture, we need leaders who are:

- willing to hold space for imperfection
- able to protect psychological safety, not just promote it
- brave enough to trade ego for empathy
- curious about their own influence.

These are the culture-shapers. They're the ones asking:

'What do people need to feel safe?'
'Where is the light leaking out of this team?'
'What does respect look like in practice?'

What It Looks Like Across the Sectors

In Facilities Management, it's the site supervisor who schedules roster flexibility for a single parent without needing to be asked.

In construction, it's the project manager who stops a concrete pour to prioritise mental health checks after a loss on site.

In demolition, it's the team leader who starts toolbox talks with 'What's one thing you're proud of this week?' before diving into hazards.

This is what happens when culture isn't driven by performance, but by presence.

When leadership stops measuring output and starts cultivating energy.

When people stop walking into work to survive – and start arriving to belong.

A Culture That Glows in the Dark

The kind of workplace culture I advocate for doesn't vanish when the CEO walks out or when targets are missed. It doesn't rely on slogans or external validation.

It lives in micro-moments. It stays.

It is carried by the quiet pride of the worker who cleans behind the scenes, the welder who teaches the apprentice without ego, the administrator who remembers everyone's birthday.

This is phosphorescent culture: human-led, values-charged, and built to last.

And once you've worked in it, you'll never want to go back.

Leadership By Luminescence: Sustaining Influence And Vision

Real leadership doesn't flash – it glows.

The workplaces of yesterday revered control. Volume. Hustle. The leader who dominated meetings, replied to emails at midnight, and wore exhaustion like a trophy was the one considered committed. That model rewarded burnout. It demanded visibility over value. And it left too many people feeling small, unseen, or afraid to fail.

But the future asks something different. It asks for luminescent leadership – the kind that radiates from within, that holds space without needing the stage, that absorbs values and vision and emits them with quiet strength. It asks for leaders who don't just command, but connect. Who don't manage for outcomes, but lead for alignment.

This is not performative leadership. It is phosphorescent. It lasts.

A Quick (and Necessary) Primer: Fixed vs Growth Mindset

Much of what we've accepted as leadership comes from a fixed mindset – the belief that talent is static, intelligence is predetermined, and effort is secondary.

Coined by psychologist Dr Carol Dweck, a fixed mindset sounds like:

'That's just how I am.'
'I'm not good at that.'
'I don't do emotions.'
'I've always led this way.'

But growth-minded leaders think differently. They see effort as essential. They view feedback as a gift. They embrace vulnerability – not as weakness, but as wisdom.

Fixed Mindset:
- talent is innate
- mistakes are shameful
- authority is preserved by being right
- safety is procedural, not emotional.

Growth Mindset:
- talent can evolve
- mistakes are feedback
- authority is built through trust
- safety is co-created, owned by the team.

Phosphorescent intelligence requires a growth mindset – not just for learning, but for leading. Because in workplaces where people are physically at risk – on demolition sites, in confined spaces, around machinery – the safest leader is not the smartest in the room. It's the one who listens hardest.

Old World vs New World Leadership

This shift is not soft. It's structural. It changes how teams interact, how safety is lived, how decisions are made, and how legacy is built.

Why This Matters in High-Risk, High-Impact Industries

In Facilities Management, construction, and demolition, leadership isn't about motivational speeches, it's about the subtle signals you send every day. Are your people bracing when you walk in? Or breathing easier?

I once worked with a project manager in demolition who stopped a high-pressure job mid-morning – not because of a technical risk, but because he sensed the crew was too emotionally depleted to be sharp. He didn't wait for an incident. He created space to rest and reset.

That's not weakness. That's wisdom.

It's also safety leadership in its purest form.

The Virtue of Sustainable Influence

This chapter is not a theory. It's a call to the kind of leadership that:

- chooses curiosity over control
- embeds empathy into every directive
- holds space for difference
- leaves light in others, not just instructions.

When leaders show up with calm, values-aligned presence, they become the steady light in an unpredictable world.

You don't have to be loud to be respected. You don't have to be perfect to be trusted. You just have to glow.

What It Looks Like On Site and In Practice

A site supervisor who checks in on a team member's family without it being 'in their remit'.

A Facilities Manager who starts each week with: 'What's one thing you need from me to do your job well?'

A demolition team leader who gives their apprentice room to fail safely – and then reflect, not retreat.

A construction director who asks for feedback, even when it's uncomfortable – especially then.

Leadership by luminescence is not about charisma. It's about consistency. It's about integrity. And it's about the willingness to go first – into honesty, into unlearning, into accountability.

The Safety Link: Your Influence Can Save a Life

In physical environments, psychological safety has a direct link to physical safety.

When leaders glow:

- workers stop pretending
- hazards are reported sooner
- fatigue is acknowledged before it becomes fatal
- people pause when they're unsure – instead of pushing through and hoping for the best.

One of the most powerful safety leaders I've met in the construction space didn't say much. But when he asked, 'How are you, really?' – he meant it. That question prevented three resignations in six months and was directly linked to a 28 percent drop in incident reports. Why?

Because people didn't fear the fallout of being human. That's leadership that glows.

And that glow multiplies.

From Fleeting Influence to Lasting Legacy

To lead this way is to move beyond managing for outcomes and start leading for impact that lasts.

Because the question is not:

'Did they follow orders?'"

It's:

'Did they feel safe?'
'Did they feel seen?'
'Did I leave them better than I found them?'

Leadership by luminescence is not about spotlight moments.

It's about who you become in the quiet. It's about who you illuminate on the way.

Introducing the Leadership Personas

To lead with glow is to lead with deep self-awareness and an unwavering commitment to psychological safety.

Through our work, we've identified three core leadership personas, each a unique expression of phosphorescent intelligence. These personas offer leaders a way to understand their natural glow style and develop it into a powerful force for team culture, cohesion, and impact.

1. The Quiet Glow Leader

This leader radiates calm and grounded energy. Their strength lies not in grand gestures, but in consistency, deep listening, and emotional steadiness. They create trust through reliability and presence, fostering environments where people feel safe to take thoughtful risks and grow at their own pace.

2. The Transformational Listener

Empathetic and highly intuitive, this leader holds space for others to rise. They do not rush to fix or advise but instead illuminate insights through intentional pauses and powerful questions. Their gift is in enabling breakthroughs and nurturing untapped potential in individuals and teams.

3. The Cultural Anchor

This leader is a stabilising force, especially in times of adversity or change. They are deeply aligned with organisational values and embody resilience. By role-modelling emotional regulation and consistency, they bind teams together and guide them through uncertainty with clarity and care.

Glow Pathways: Developing Your Persona

Each leadership persona has a developmental arc – what we call a 'Glow Pathway'. These pathways are not rigid or fixed. Rather, they are reflective and adaptive, encouraging leaders to grow into their strengths while expanding their capacity in areas that feel less natural.

Key elements of every Glow Pathway include:

- **Emotional Intelligence Expansion:** strengthening empathy, emotional regulation, and relational awareness.

- **Communication Depth:** developing authenticity, clarity, and calm in verbal and non-verbal communication.

- **Self-Awareness and Reflection:** engaging in regular self-check-ins to illuminate blind spots and sustain presence.

- **Psychological Safety Practices:** creating spaces of permission, non-judgment, and trust for all team members.

Each leader may resonate with one persona more than the others, but mastery comes through understanding all three – and knowing when to draw on each. In today's complex workplace environments, adaptability and depth are the new leadership edge.

Person-Centric Business Models: Putting People At The Heart Of Growth

This isn't a trend. It's a return to truth.

There was a time when 'people-first' lived quietly in mission statements, squeezed somewhere between 'integrity' and 'excellence.' But no more. In today's workplaces, especially in high-pressure, high-turnover environments like Facilities Management, construction, and demolition, person-centric leadership is not a bonus – it's the baseline.

And not because it sounds good. Because it works. When you build around people, you unlock performance. You build resilience. You create workplaces that don't just function – but flourish.

Person-Centric Is Not Just 'HR'

This is not about fruit bowls or a laminated set of values in the tearoom.

It's about:

- designing policies that flex around people instead of forcing people to flex around policies
- understanding that what feels safe for one team member might overwhelm another
- making room for real feedback, even when it's messy
- listening to the quietest voices on the site, not just the most confident ones in the meeting.

In Facilities Management, it looks like giving frontline staff the tools – and the time – to report safety issues without fear.

In construction, it's rethinking rostering to reduce burnout and boost mental clarity on site.

In demolition, it's creating clear communication pathways for neurodivergent workers who may not speak up in group settings, but still have something important to say.

Phosphorescent intelligence thrives in these environments because it doesn't just see workers. It sees people. It sees complexity. It sees potential.

Change Is Not Just Possible – It's Imperative

We have to stop pretending that high turnover, disengagement, and burnout are 'just part of the job'. They're not the norm. They're the warning signs.

Too often, we normalise dysfunction.

We call it resilience. We call it industry standard. We call it hard work.

But the reality is, when people are undervalued, everything suffers. Culture breaks. Safety erodes. Trust disappears. And good people leave.

The businesses that are brave enough to recalibrate – to listen, learn, and evolve – don't just retain staff. They lead. I've worked with companies that reduced staff churn from 35 percent to under 10 in less than a year. Not through perks or gimmicks, but through deep human engagement. Through checking in, not checking boxes.

What Person-Centric Really Looks Like

A cleaner with English as a second language is offered audio training tailored to their pace – not handed a 45-page PDF.

A single parent on a demolition crew is asked, 'What does flexibility look like for you?' – not given a generic hybrid policy.

A neurodivergent team member in a construction firm is invited to submit feedback post-meeting – so their insights aren't lost in a fast-paced discussion.

This isn't over-engineering. This is overdue empathy. This is what it means to glow at the systems level.

The Ripple Effect of Empowered People

When people feel seen, safe, and supported, they don't just show up.

They rise.

Innovation increases – because ideas are welcomed, not shut down.

Loyalty deepens – because people feel a sense of belonging.

Safety improves – because people are mentally present, not emotionally surviving.

Pride grows – because people feel aligned with what they do and who they do it for.

And let's be clear: people who are proud of where they work don't just stay.

They advocate. They recruit. They protect the brand from the inside out.

From Management to Stewardship

The shift isn't just structural – it's spiritual.

Person-centric leadership is about moving from control to care, from oversight to insight. It's about asking:

'Who do you want to become here?'
'What does growth look like for you?'
'How can we design a workplace that lets you shine – and encourages you to stay?'

Because when people are held, they don't just perform. They transform.

And when they transform, the business grows – ethically, sustainably, and exponentially.

The Business Model of the Future

It's not extractive. It's not transactional. And it's not fragile.

It is steady. Regenerative. Scalable. Human.

Where people aren't treated as 'assets', but as the very reason the business exists. Where metrics matter, but never more than meaning. Where heart becomes your greatest competitive edge.

At the core of the person-centric model lies the concept of growth culture: not as a buzzword, but as a deeply embedded system in which both business and humanity are nurtured to grow together.

Person-centric isn't fluff. It's foundational.

It's how you glow, grow, and go the distance.

A Regenerative Circle: Built Around Growth Culture

Unlike traditional linear structures, this model is circular and holistic. It mirrors how sustainable businesses operate in the real world – interconnected, adaptive, and evolving.

1. **Guiding Principles: The Heartbeat of Growth**

These are more than just words on a wall. They are the living essence of the organisation.

- Purpose defines why the business exists.
- Vision articulates where it is heading.
- Values determine how people behave, especially when no one is watching.

These are the compass points that guide every action. They shape how individuals show up, how decisions are made, and how leaders navigate times of clarity and uncertainty alike.

2. **Framework and Narrative: Your Story and Strategy**

A business must know not only what it does, but why it matters.

- **Strategy** is more than a plan. It is the articulation of how the organisation aspires to win – ethically, authentically, and with heart.
- **Market context** is an ongoing awareness of the external world and a readiness to respond with relevance.
- **Brand** is the outward reflection of inner truths – the message and meaning the business conveys to the world.

This is the point where metrics meet meaning, where growth is not manufactured but cultivated through trust and clarity.

3. Organic Growth: Culture That Moves

Culture is not a static concept – it is *alive*.

- **Behaviours** are the everyday patterns that either reinforce or weaken cultural values.
- **Communication** and **engagement** determine the extent to which people feel included, heard, and aligned with the broader purpose.

True growth is not imposed. It is generated through consistency, integrity, and connection. When these factors align, positive culture becomes a force of momentum, not maintenance.

4. Key Influences: The Human Engine

This model recognises that systems alone do not create success – people do.

- **Leadership** in this model is servant-led, emotionally intelligent, and rooted in impact on people.
- **The working environment** must be psychologically safe, inclusive, and energising – not merely functional.
- **Policies** and **processes** are not constraints but enablers.

The model is designed to empower rather than control, to support rather than obstruct.

Where human systems and operational systems meet, there is the potential for real transformation.

Person-Centric Is Not a Luxury – It Is a Foundation

This is not about referring to people as 'resources'. It is about recognising that people are the very reason the business exists in the first place. It is through this lens that resilient organisations not only survive – they evolve, adapt, and expand their potential.

The person-centric model is scalable because it is sustainable. It is competitive because it is built on trust. It is future-ready because it prioritises humanity.

Where Heart Becomes the Strategic Advantage

In this future-focused model:

- People are not merely engaged – they are inspired.
- Processes are not simply followed – they are elevated.
- Growth is not limited to financial performance – it is cultural, emotional, and purposeful.

Because when growth culture is person-centred, success is no longer measured only by how far you go, but by how deeply you grow – together.

The Business Model of The Future

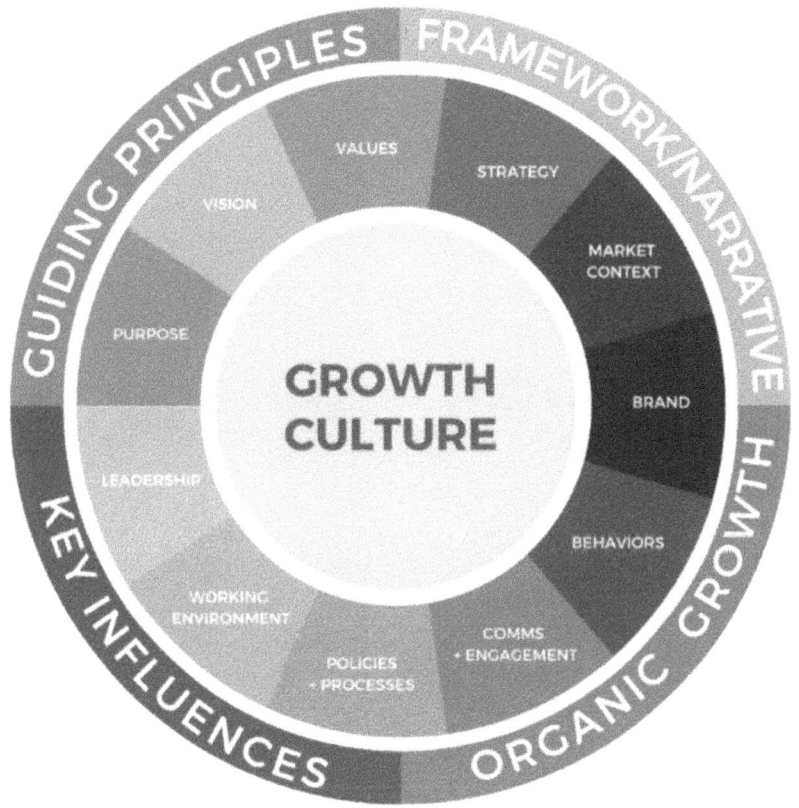

HOLISTIC GROWTH SOLUTIONS - HOLISTIC GROWTH MODEL

Beyond Survival:
The Economics of Thriving

Beyond Survival: The Economics of Thriving

What if the greatest opportunity for growth wasn't found in another system, sales playbook, or strategic hire – but in the heartbeat of your culture? What if light itself could become your most powerful asset?

This chapter meets you at a critical juncture. By now, you've journeyed through the psychological seasons, the regenerative rhythms, and the quiet strength of phosphorescent intelligence. You've seen the necessity of rest as strategy, safety as performance infrastructure, and reflection as fuel for innovation.

Now, we shift. From internal recognition to external expression. From theory to economic clarity. From soul to system.

In boardrooms, breakrooms, and behind closed doors, a reckoning has begun. Leaders who once equated success with speed, productivity with pressure, and culture with slogans are now feeling the tremor of truth rumble beneath their foundations. Something is breaking. And something luminous is pushing through.

The last few years have revealed what many hoped to avoid: the old models don't work anymore. Workplaces that ran on fear, competition, and control may have once delivered results – but at what cost?

Burnout is no longer a badge of honour. Disconnection is not a necessary evil. And culture, it turns out, is not a soft thing. It is the infrastructure that determines whether people stay, thrive, and grow – or silently exit.

This time, it must be different. Not because the moral case isn't enough – it is. But because the business case is now undeniable. There is no separation between wellbeing and performance. There is no path to long-term profitability that bypasses human sustainability.

The Glow Advantage: Culture That Pays Back

For decades, profit and wellbeing were framed as competing priorities. But data now tells another story: workplaces that embed care, rhythm, and reflective leadership don't just feel better – they perform better.

According to Deloitte, companies with strong wellbeing cultures see up to 41 percent lower turnover and 83 percent fewer sick days. Harvard Business Review notes that every $1 invested in mental health and wellbeing yields a return of $4 to $6. McKinsey reports that toxic workplace culture is 10.4 times more predictive of attrition than compensation.

These aren't guesses. These are the economic signals of a new paradigm:

- SecureTel saw a 27 percent drop in voluntary turnover after implementing a cultural reset based on psychological safety and rhythm.

- A mid-sized Facilities Management organisation embedded the GLOW Toolkit and saw a 16 percent increase in revenue in under 12 months.

- One team's daily 'Mental Health Pulse Checks' reduced insurance premiums after it measurably reduced incidents.

The Human Operating System

Phosphorescent intelligence is a reawakening, a rewiring of how we work, live, and thrive.

We are not designed for constant push. We are built for cycles – rest, renewal, reflection, response. High-performing teams honour this. They create rituals. They build rhythm. They don't just work – they pulse.

Our nervous systems flourish in psychologically safe spaces. Our creativity blooms when feedback is welcomed, not weaponised. Our loyalty deepens not through pay increases alone, but through meaning, belonging, and belief in the future we're building.

Burnout is not the price of greatness. It's the invoice from a system designed to extract.

Phosphorescent intelligence offers the alternative:

- cultures grounded in light-sharing leadership
- performance frameworks built on reflection, not just reaction
- work rhythms that follow psychological seasons
- decisions that regenerate, not deplete.

This isn't just good for people. It's good for business. Because healthy systems create healthy outcomes.

And when we nurture the conditions in which humans can truly thrive, innovation emerges, performance accelerates, and trust compounds into loyalty.

Why Now: The Cost of Delay

Every moment spent in a system of survival carries compounding costs:

- **Legal risk:** psychological injury claims can cost upward of $350,000 per incident.
- **Attrition:** replacing one experienced employee can cost 1.5-2x their salary.
- **Brand risk:** culture is now visible. Platforms like Glassdoor, LinkedIn, and industry whisper networks amplify internal dynamics externally.

- **Lost momentum:** each delay in cultural reform is a delay in performance potential.

The organisations that act now will win:
- in reputation
- in resilience
- in revenue.

Because culture is not a cost centre. It is performance infrastructure.

And phosphorescent intelligence is not a theory. It's a commercial strategy with a human soul.

A Call to Light: This is the Shift of Our Time

We are not here to tweak what's broken. We are here to reimagine what's possible.

This is our invitation to redesign work that reflects who we are at our best. To replace reaction with rhythm. Strain with sustainability. Power with presence.

The future will not belong to the loudest or fastest. It will belong to those who lead with light.

Phosphorescent intelligence is the framework. The GLOW Toolkit is the method. The Growth Culture Roadmap is your path forward.

So if you're wondering what comes next – this is it. The practices, rituals, and rhythms you've already seen are not just ideas. They are building blocks. And the next chapter offers the full architecture.

This time, it must be different. Because this time, we know better. Because this time, the cost of doing nothing is too high. Because this time, it isn't just about survival. It's about building brilliance that lasts.

So start where you are.
Reclaim your rhythm.
Design the glow.
Lead with light.
Glow forward.

The Growth Mindset: Sustaining Long-Term Success

This is not about hype. This is about becoming. Let's cut to it: the world doesn't need more 'high performers' operating on survival mode.

It needs real humans – resilient, curious, unafraid to unlearn – who can bend without breaking, stumble without shame, and stretch into newness with soul.

That's what a growth mindset offers. And when paired with phosphorescent intelligence, it becomes unstoppable.

What Is a Growth Mindset, Really? (And Why Does It Matter Now?)

A growth mindset is the belief that abilities and intelligence can be developed through effort, feedback, and learning.

It's the opposite of the fixed mindset, which tells us:

'I'm just not good at that.'
'That's above my pay grade.'
'I failed, so I'm not cut out for this.'

But in a growth mindset world, failure becomes fuel. Effort becomes power. And feedback becomes a gift, not a threat. In workplaces rooted in phosphorescent intelligence, growth mindset isn't optional – it's the cultural oxygen. It's how we breathe through disruption and come out not just intact – but transformed.

The Link Between Glowing and Growing

Phosphorescence is the glow that stays after the light is gone.

Growth mindset is the belief that we can still shine – even after we've stumbled, stretched, or been cracked open.

These two concepts are sisters. Together, they create organisations that:

- reward learning, not just knowing
- see vulnerability as strength
- build cultures where failure is data, not damnation
- celebrate process over perfection.

I've worked with leaders who started off terrified of feedback – and who now invite it before every quarterly review. I've seen teams go from paralysed by risk to energised by experimentation.

This is not a fairy tale. This is the ripple effect of belief.

From Rigid Roots to Regenerative Culture

Growth mindset challenges everything the old system taught us:

- that leaders must have all the answers
- that mistakes are embarrassing
- that speed matters more than depth.

In this phosphorescent world we're building?

- Leaders ask, 'What did we learn?' before 'What did we lose?'
- Teams are safe to experiment – even when they don't succeed.
- Hiring focuses on humility, curiosity, and coachability over pedigree.

This isn't soft. It's scalable. And it works.

Case Study: When Curiosity Outpaced Perfection

One mid-sized Facilities Management business I partnered with was stuck in a productivity rut. Every new process was met with groans. Staff avoided suggesting ideas because the last one that failed led to a public scolding.

So we flipped the script.

We launched a Glow & Grow board:

'Glow' for what we tried that worked.

'Grow' for what we tried that didn't – but taught us something.

Within 90 days, idea submissions had increased by 370 percent and a cleaner had suggested a change to site entry protocols that saved $28,000/year.

The culture had shifted from fear to fuel.

All because the team no longer feared being wrong. They were invited to be real.

The Glow That Doesn't Burn Out

Growth mindset is sustainable because it isn't based on hype or hustle.

It's based on hope.

And hope, when embedded into workplace DNA, is what creates resilience – not just as a survival trait, but as a strategic advantage.

A growth mindset says:

'This challenge is here to grow me.'

'I haven't mastered this . . . yet.'

'I don't fear feedback – I crave it.'

When organisations reflect this, they become regenerative systems.

They don't just survive change – they shape it.

To the Brave Ones Driving This Forward

You don't need a title to champion a growth mindset. You need conviction. And maybe, just maybe, the courage to go first.

To admit what you don't know.

To try something wild and wonderful.

To ask, 'What if we could do it differently?'

That's the glow. That's the growth. That's the future of work.

Real Stories, Real Fire

A construction firm introduced mental health first responders – not to tick a box, but because two team members were almost lost to suicide.

Since then, absenteeism dropped by 40 percent, and site supervisors are now requesting empathy training.

A senior leader finally spoke about their battle with chronic pain during a team meeting. One sentence. That was it. The following week, three staff came forward asking for flexible work – and for the first time, they were heard without judgment.

An introverted team member, often overlooked in meetings, was given a space to submit thoughts post-discussion. Six months later, their ideas led to a new client onboarding model that increased satisfaction by 18 percent.

When we make room for the whole person, whole cultures begin to heal.

This Isn't Fluffy – It's the Future of Work

The research is already there:

- companies with inclusive cultures are 6 times more innovative (Deloitte)
- diverse teams outperform homogenous ones by 35 percent in problem-solving (McKinsey)
- teams with high psychological safety have 27 percent lower turnover, 76 percent more engagement, and 50 percent more productivity (Google's Project Aristotle).

But stats don't move hearts.

Stories do. Compassion does. Courage does.

And we need all three now – not later, not after the next review cycle – now.

From Performative to Transformative

Ask yourself:

Does our culture invite difference – or just tolerate it?

Do we co-design solutions with those impacted?

Do our leaders see equity work as a competency, not just a cause?

Because inclusion is not a department. It's a verb.

And holistic wellbeing is its foundation.

To the Reader With Power: Use It

If you have a budget – redirect it.

If you have influence – amplify unheard voices.

If you've made mistakes – own them, and grow forward.

If you're unsure – ask better questions, not louder ones.

Because nothing changes without you. It's not just up to the CEO, or the people team. It's up to you – reading this. Feeling the tension. Wanting to do better.

Let this chapter not just inform you. Let it move you.

Let's Build the Culture We've All Been Waiting For

One where difference is celebrated. One where adaptation is the default. One where healing, growth, and innovation are intertwined.

Not just for this generation – but for the ones watching quietly, hoping someone will finally light the way.

Tools and Frameworks for Implementation

It's time to move from admiration to application. From inspiration to integration.

From glow as a concept to glow as a system.

Phosphorescent intelligence was never meant to stay in theory. It belongs in your policies, team meetings, metrics, inductions, and even your safety audits. It should show up in moments of quiet leadership and in high-pressure environments. On the ground and in the boardroom.

This chapter gives you the how.

Not a one-size-fits-all manual. But adaptable, human-first tools – designed to flex with your workplace's real-world challenges and rhythms.

These are frameworks we've embedded with cleaning teams, construction crews, FM managers, and C-suite leaders alike. And they work.

Tool 1: The Phosphorescent Culture Diagnostic

A 20-minute audit designed to measure depth, not just surface culture.

Five Dimensions

Safety: do people feel safe to speak up, break down, or raise concerns without retribution?

Visibility: who gets seen, heard, and elevated – and who doesn't?

Wellbeing: is care embedded into systems, or performative and seasonal?

Growth: are learning and failure part of the rhythm, or reserved for the few?

Legacy: if your culture had a voice, what would it say when no one's watching?

How to Use

Run this with your leadership team every six months. Rate each area from 1 to 5.

If your total score is under 15, you don't need surface tweaks. You need a culture reset.

Tool 2: The Glow & Grow Review Model

This replaces the performance review nobody looks forward to.

It centres real experience, feedback, reflection, and potential.

Ask your team:

- What made you glow this quarter?
- Where did you grow?
- What felt misaligned or murky?
- What's one thing we can shift to help you shine more sustainably?

How to Use

Pair this with peer feedback and allow the person time to reflect privately before your check-in.

Works across industries – from field staff to admin to executive roles.

Bonus: use this at toolbox talks or monthly site reviews – it builds trust and ownership.

Framework 3: The Phosphorescent Leadership Model

Not a style. A stance.

Four Anchors

Presence: I see you.

Curiosity: I don't need to know everything.

Compassionate Accountability: I'll hold you and the goal.
Regenerative Energy: I don't burn out to look strong.

Monthly pulse check for leaders:

- Where am I leading from burnout instead of belief?
- Where am I glowing?
- Where am I leaking light?

This is your leadership immune system. Use it to build trust and emotional safety around you.

Tool 4: The Person-Centric Strategy Canvas

Designed to replace rigid strategy templates with something living, human, and responsive.

Five Components

People: who are they? What do they value, fear, and dream of?

Purpose: what are we actually here to do, beyond profit?

Practices: are our systems reinforcing or resisting our purpose?

Patterns: what invisible behaviours are shaping our culture?

Power: who holds it? How is it used? Who gets left out?

When to Use

During annual strategy sessions, contract transitions, or after a cultural incident. **This strategy canvas** works especially well in construction and Facilities Management environments undergoing rapid change.

Warning: this may challenge long-protected assumptions!

Glowstorming Sessions

Ditch the brainstorm. This is different.

Quarterly Glowstorm

Set the space (physical or virtual) so it feels safe, not sterile. Ask the team:

- What's dimming our light?
- What's igniting it?
- What rules are we keeping that we should have outgrown?
- Don't rush. Sit with the answers. Co-create change.

Result: teams that run regular glowstorms report a 31 percent increase in innovation, higher team cohesion, fewer passive-aggressive behaviours, and fewer missed signals.

Tool 5: The Integration Playbook Builder

Every organisation is at a different stage. Use these three tracks to meet your team where they are.

Each track includes:

- a 90-day roadmap

- progress markers (yes, stories count)
- human-first indicators of success
- optional support plans for teams with limited internal capacity.

This Chapter is a Call to Everyone

Don't wait for permission.
Don't wait for the right budget cycle.
Don't wait for it to come from the top.

If you're a team leader – run a Glow & Grow.
If you're a supervisor – pilot the Culture Diagnostic.
If you're in the C-suite – adopt the Leadership Model as your compass.
If you're on the tools – bring glow into your next safety meeting.

You don't have to overhaul everything at once. You just have to *choose to glow*.

Because phosphorescent intelligence isn't just felt. It's built.

And now, you've got the blueprint.

Glow and Grow Toolkit

Half price discount code GLOW50

Real Stories, Real Fire

This chapter isn't just a series of examples. It's a reckoning. A reminder. A revelation.

Because no matter how strong a model or how clear a strategy, what moves people is proof. Not theoretical proof. Lived proof.

So when someone asks me, 'But does this actually work?', I don't reach for data first.

I reach for people.

I reach for stories of the cleaners, the construction workers, the middle managers, the directors who finally exhaled when they were given permission to care – and to be cared for.

These are the people who proved that glow is not a metaphor. It's a movement. And it's happening.

Case Study 1: The Cleaning Crew That Became Culture Champions

A national Facilities Management company was facing a revolving door on its frontline. Recruitment was constant. Retention was collapsing. Leadership assumed the issue was pay.

But after three weeks of shadowing, listening, and observing, what we heard was something else entirely.

They didn't feel seen.

No eye contact during handovers. No voice in team briefings. No acknowledgment of their value.

So we flipped the hierarchy.

Frontline staff began opening team meetings with site updates. We created a new role: 'Dignity Advocates', internal reps responsible for collecting feedback and ensuring rest breaks,

PPE access, and respect. Each cleaner was asked: 'What would make you proud to work here?'

Six months later:

- turnover dropped 63 percent
- engagement scores rose from 29 to 82 percent
- clients noticed the difference and began complimenting team morale
- staff began referring friends – not for the paycheck, but for the culture.

That's what happens when glow becomes embedded. Pride becomes performance.

And the cleaners become the culture.

Case Study 2: The Leader Who Chose Vulnerability Over Control

A senior executive in construction – respected, results-driven, but distant – came to one of our leadership retreats. Arms crossed. Posture stiff. Twenty years of KPIs wrapped around his body like armour.

Until one moment cracked it.

'I don't know how to lead anymore. The old way made me feel powerful, but it made me lonely. I want to try something else.'

That moment changed everything.

He asked his team to anonymously rate his leadership. He paused all new initiatives for three months and entered a 'silent listening' window. He met one-on-one with every staff member – and just listened.

Twelve months on:

- psychological safety soared to 91 percent
- innovation metrics doubled
- he became the most requested internal mentor across the business.

He later told me, 'I've led hundreds of projects. But for the first time in my career, I feel human again.'

That's glow.

Not loud. But lasting.

Case Study 3: From Burnout to Beacon – Rebuilding After the Breaking Point

A mid-sized consultancy came to us post-crisis. Staff were exhausted. Leadership turnover was rampant. The brand was bleeding credibility and talent.

We didn't offer a flashy intervention. We introduced a phosphorescent framework.

Step by step, we:

- embedded mental health first responders
- introduced the Glow & Grow board in every department
- paused performance reviews and replaced them with monthly coaching check-ins
- rebuilt metrics to include curiosity, collaboration, and psychological safety.

Twelve months later:

- revenue increased 16 percent
- Employee Net Promoter Score jumped from -17 to +53
- and the business was listed in a national 'Best Places to Work' feature for the first time.

And most importantly? The culture didn't bounce back. It rebuilt – differently.

Stronger. More human.

These Stories Aren't Outliers. They're Leading Indicators.

What they show is clear:

Dignity drives retention.
Psychological safety drives performance.
Connection drives innovation.
Listening drives leadership.

This isn't theory. It's already happening – on job sites, in cleaning teams, in boardrooms, and in back offices.

And it's not just possible. It's scalable.

When you:

- design policies around human life
- promote leaders who listen, not just direct
- build safety that includes emotional safety
- hire for empathy, curiosity, and courage,

You build workplaces that glow without burnout.

You turn culture from an expense into a differentiator.

Let This Chapter Be a Mirror and a Map

If you lead, ask your team: 'Where are we glowing? And where are we dimming?'

Sit in the silence that follows. Don't defend. Listen. Then act. If you don't lead (yet):

- start the conversation your team is avoiding
- be the one who brings the feedback, gently but bravely
- refuse to go dim just because others do.

Because you don't need a title to spark transformation. You just need conviction – and a willingness to go first.

Phosphorescent intelligence isn't mine to keep. It's yours to carry.

It's already working. Now it's waiting for you.

Glow Across Industries (Sidebar)

Phosphorescent intelligence was born in the high-pressure, fast-paced realities of Facilities Management and construction – sectors often overlooked in conversations about leadership and culture. However, its principles are universal. Glow is not industry-specific; it is human- specific. This chapter extends the framework into diverse sectors to demonstrate its adaptability and relevance.

Healthcare: Healing the Healers

Emotional burnout among nurses, paramedics, and hospital staff has reached crisis levels in recent years. In one regional hospital, Glowstorming was introduced to daily huddles within surgical teams. The practice enabled staff to decompress, share openly, and recognise each other's strengths. After twelve weeks, surveys reported a 34 percent improvement in team cohesion, with notable drops in reported stress levels and interpersonal tension.

Technology: Reconnecting Remote Teams

In the tech sector, isolation and disconnection are silent killers of collaboration. A global software development company embedded Glowstarter questions into their remote agile stand-ups and Slack workflows. By fostering structured yet authentic check-ins, the company saw a 22 percent boost in psychological safety scores and an 18 percent reduction in project delays attributed to team friction.

Education: Psychological Safety in Learning Environments

A high school principal implemented phosphorescent principles with faculty leadership teams, adapting them for classroom pedagogy. Educators reported feeling more empowered to admit challenges, ask for support, and test new ideas without fear of judgement. Students also benefited: surveys showed a 40 percent increase in perceived safety and engagement. Glow helped shift the culture from performance pressure to connected learning.

Beyond the Sectors: A Universal Invitation

Whether on a hospital ward, a Zoom call, or in a classroom, glow has the power to illuminate. Its relevance lies not in the sector, but in the need to build workplaces where presence, care, and human dignity are non-negotiables. Let this be an invitation to any leader, in any industry, to begin.

The Workplaces of Tomorrow are Already Being Built Today

The workplaces of tomorrow are already rising – in quiet ways, in unexpected places.

In the Facilities Management teams that choose to check in before clocking on.

In the demolition crews that hold as much space for wellbeing as they do safety.

In the construction sites that embed reflection, rest, and regenerative leadership into every layer of their scaffolding.

We are not imagining this future. We are building it.

It is happening – in every courageous decision to slow down, listen harder, and lead with heart.

These workplaces are not led by the loudest voices. They are built by the most consistent ones.

By those who model calm when stress spikes. By those who ask better questions. By those who choose care without needing credit.

These Are Person-Centric Workplaces

They no longer treat people as cogs in a productivity machine.

They design work around the human experience – respecting energy, values, neurodiversity, and life beyond the shift.

Schedules flex where they can. Feedback flows both ways. And individuality is not just tolerated – it is welcomed.

These Are Trauma-Aware Workplaces

They acknowledge that humans bring their full lives to work.

That behind every delay, every frustration, every mistake – there is often a story.

In these workplaces:

- mental health is not a side conversation
- burnout is not glorified
- empathy is not optional – it's embedded.

Supervisors are trained to notice the signs. Managers are encouraged to lead with honesty. Team members are invited to show up as they are, not just as they're expected to be.

This doesn't mean work stops. It means people stop hiding.

Systems of Trust, Not Just Efficiency

Efficiency matters. But not at the cost of trust.

The workplaces of tomorrow don't chase speed at the expense of depth.

They don't ignore the ripple effects of rushed decisions, neglected wellbeing, or unspoken exhaustion.

They understand that culture is not just what you say – it's what you model.

And the best systems? They are the ones people believe in, not just follow.

'I Don't Know, But I'm Listening'

These are not perfect workplaces. They are honest ones. In the sites and offices of the future, leaders don't pretend to have it all figured out.

They create space to learn. They share power. They co-create solutions.

It's no longer about having answers. It's about having integrity.

Valuing Process As Much As Performance

In these workplaces, leaders know that how something is done matters as much as what gets done.

They slow down enough to reflect.

They respect the rhythm of real work – not just the results on paper.

They allow space for experimentation, iteration, and failure that teaches.

Because the fastest route to results without care isn't strategy.

It's short-termism. And they know better.

Treating Wellbeing as Infrastructure

Not a theme for Mental Health Week. Not a break-room poster.

Not a reaction to a resignation or a crisis.

Wellbeing is built into every layer:

- from pre-starts to post-projects
- from contracts to culture reviews
- from onboarding to offboarding.

It is embedded, not bolted on.

And it's treated as a foundation, not a fringe benefit.

Lighting Up the Future

These are the workplaces where people don't just stay.

They thrive.
They lead.
They grow into themselves and each other.

Because when people feel seen, safe, and supported, they don't just comply – they care. They don't just produce – they protect. They don't just deliver – they innovate.

These workplaces aren't fantasy. They're emerging.

Quietly. Powerfully. Persistently.

And the leaders building them?

They aren't waiting for someone else to go first. They are the first.

These Workplaces Are Not Waiting for Change

They are choosing to be the change. One conversation, one framework, one cultural pulse at a time.

And they are lighting the way for others to follow.

Embedding Glow Through the Holistic Growth Hub

Embedding glow is not about adding more to the noise. It's about recalibrating how we measure, develop, and protect what truly matters in the workplace. It's about allowing the systems that hold us to also heal us. Glow doesn't sit on top of strategy – it seeps through it.

That's why the Holistic Growth Hub was created – not as a product, but as a possibility.

This platform is not here to impress, but to equip. To quietly support those leading from the middle. To illuminate pathways for those tasked with building culture when the manual doesn't exist.

The Hub is how organisations begin to speak glow fluently.

The Holistic Growth Hub: A Living System of Support

The Holistic Growth Hub exists as a dynamic, human-centred ecosystem designed to make glow a lived reality. It doesn't require you to discard your current structure. It invites you to rewire it with integrity.

It's a toolkit, a companion, a cultural compass. It's where KPIs become compassionate. Where safety becomes relational. Where learning becomes personal. Where performance doesn't just measure effort – but meaning.

Key Features Rooted in Purpose, Not Performance

- **Psychosocial Foundations:** templates, reflections, and self-guided audits designed to align seamlessly with ISO 45003 and WHS requirements – turning compliance into care.

- **Emotional Climate Insights:** facilitated team check-ins and emotional literacy tools help leaders detect the emotional pulse before burnout arrives.

- **Leadership Activation Tools:** glow personas, conversation guides, and coaching resources foster depth, not just direction.

- **Cultural Shaping Resources:** language templates, rituals, and embedded micro-practices support a tone of trust across departments.

- **Progress Reflection Prompts:** instead of dashboards filled with noise, the Hub encourages meaningful check-ins that allow teams to sense, reflect, and re-centre.

'The Hub is not a replacement for leadership – it's a reflection tool for it.'

Real-World Proof: The SecureTel Case

When SecureTel integrated the Holistic Growth Hub into its leadership and training systems:

- 100 percent of people leaders completed emotional safety onboarding
- voluntary turnover dropped by 27 percent in six months
- psychological safety check-ins averaged a score of 9.2/10.

Glow became visible – not in posters, but in people.

Designed With Leaders, Not Just For Them

Unlike generic platforms engineered by coders, the Holistic Growth Hub was crafted by organisational wellbeing strategists and people practitioners who understand the realities of risk, leadership, and emotional labour. It speaks the language of job sites, offices, crew rooms, and boardrooms.

Not a Platform – A Philosophy in Practice

This isn't just an app to download. It's an embodiment of a deeper truth: that when leaders tend to the emotional architecture of work, everything changes.

Glow, at scale, is not a dream. It's a design.

So whether you build your own internal system or adopt the Holistic Growth Hub, let this be the moment you stop treating wellbeing as something extra.

Because when glow is embedded – genuinely, courageously, systemically – organisations don't just work.

They shine.

Further Reading & Resources

Holistic Growth Hub

Unlock the next level of your leadership journey.

Scan here to access premium resources, exclusive frameworks, and confidential tools designed for transformative change.

Dare to Lead Differently—Become a Member Today!

Note: Access is reserved for subscribers and clients—scan to learn more and join the Holistic Growth Hub community.

Epilogue: The Manifesto of the Glowing Ones

Epilogue: The Manifesto of the Glowing Ones

For those who stayed.
For those who stayed soft.
For those who stayed luminous – even when the world told them to dim.

This isn't a conclusion. It's a continuation.

A manifesto. A mirror. A remembering.

This book wasn't written from a pedestal. It was written from the floor.

From early mornings on forgotten job sites.

From whispered one-on-ones with leaders too burnt out to speak their truth.

From demolition yards and Facilities Management offices, where silence carried more truth than noise ever could.

This didn't come from a business plan.

It came from every moment I stood in the shadow of a system that said, 'Push harder,' and asked instead, 'What if we paused?'

It came from watching a cleaner arrive an hour early just to feel calm.

From the project lead who stayed after a meeting, not to talk – but to be present.

From the manager who looked down during a review and murmured, 'I'm not sure who I'm becoming here . . . '

Let Me Be Clear

I don't glow because the world has been gentle. I glow because I refused to let it dim me.

And if you've read this far, then something in you glows too.

Maybe it's faint. Maybe it's buried. Maybe it's just flickering again.

But it's there.

And now, you get to choose what to do with it.

The Invitation to Build

Let's build what should have always existed.

A workplace that doesn't extract – but expands.

A culture that doesn't demand perfection – but honours process.

A system that doesn't just survive – but heals, adapts, and elevates.

Yes, it will be hard.

Yes, the old ways will knock, over and over. Yes, you may be misunderstood.

But your glow is your resistance. Your integrity is your strategy.

Your care will fuel this revolution.

Our Blueprint: The Growth Culture Framework

At Holistic Growth Solutions, we believe workplaces don't change by accident. They change by design.

That's why we created the Holistic Growth Model – a person-centric, psychologically safe, and regenerative framework that helps businesses navigate the evolving complexity of today's workforce.

This model draws upon workplace psychology, leadership development, and HR excellence – integrating emotional intelligence, trauma-aware practice, systems thinking, and sustainable growth.

At the heart of the model sits our Growth Culture Framework, a dynamic blueprint for real-world transformation. It centres growth not just as a metric, but as a mindset, a muscle, and a movement.

Here's what it encompasses:

Guiding Principles

Purpose, Vision, Values: your foundation. These aren't words on a wall. They're your roots.

Framework and Narrative

Strategy, Market Context, Brand: how you tell your story, how you adapt, how you align. This is your orientation.

Organic Growth

Behaviours, Communication, Engagement: your cultural pulse. This is how growth lives in your day-to-day.

Key Influences

Leadership, Environment, Policy, Process: your infrastructure. The system behind the soul.

At the Centre, Growth Culture

Not hype-driven, but human-led. Not performative, but purpose-built. Not fragile, but fiercely resilient.

This framework is not theoretical. It's practical. It can be implemented, evolved, and measured.

It's already being used to transform workplaces in Facilities Management, construction, demolition, and beyond.

It's the map forward.

For leaders ready to lead differently. For teams ready to rise.

For businesses ready to thrive – with care as their competitive edge.

This Is the Shift That's Already Happening

The workplaces of tomorrow are already being built – quietly, intentionally, bravely.

They are:

- **Person-Centric** – seeing people as whole humans, not cogs.
- **Trauma-Aware** – leading with compassion, not compliance.
- **Integrity-Driven** – building trust through presence, not pressure.
- **Growth-Aligned** – scaling care and strategy side by side.

They treat wellbeing as infrastructure.

They prioritise how something is done just as much as what gets done.

They don't just adapt – they regenerate.

This isn't a cultural shift. It's a business revolution.

Why This Isn't 'Soft' Work – It's Strategic

Phosphorescent workplaces are:

- **more productive** – because people feel safe
- **more innovative** – because feedback is welcome
- **more resilient** – because people burn bright, not out
- **more profitable** – because aligned people outperform afraid people.

This isn't about 'making work nicer'.

It's about making it work – ethically, sustainably, humanly.

Bringing Glow to Life: The Growth Culture Roadmap
Embedding Phosphorescent Intelligence into the Everyday

Phosphorescent intelligence is not just an idea. It is a living, breathing culture. It is the quiet strength that moves through workplaces where people are seen, not spent. Where leaders glow without burning out. Where teams flourish through rhythm, not rush.

We have journeyed together through the depth and detail of glow. Now, this roadmap is your bridge from insight to impact.

This is not a checklist. This is cultural choreography. This is how we align the pulse of a workplace with its purpose. This is how we centre wellbeing not as a department, but as infrastructure. This is how we stop seeing care and performance as opposites – and start realising they are co-authors of legacy.

Each phase of this roadmap is grounded in the phosphorescent frameworks already explored. It draws from the psychology of rhythm, the science of performance, and the soul of what it means to lead with light. The roadmap integrates the GLOW Toolkit – the practical framework introduced throughout this book – and invites you to live it into being. Make the commitment, and let this be your compass.

Phase 1: ALIGN
Establish Meaning, Rhythm and Resonance

- Reconnect to Purpose.
  - » Begin not with goals, but with grounding. Ask: Why do we exist beyond profit? What legacy do we want to leave behind?

- Clarify a Vision That Glows.
  - » Your vision must hold both your commercial ambition and your cultural heartbeat. Make it human. Make it heard.

- Transform Values into Verbs.
  - » Values without behaviours are poetry without voice. Define what your values look, sound, and feel like in daily action.

Glow Lens: this phase reflects the psychological seasons and the power of personal leadership clarity. It anchors every strategy in the heartbeat of why.

Profit Lens: organisations with clear alignment experience lower attrition, higher engagement, and faster decision-making. A culture aligned is a business accelerated.

Phase 2: EMBED
Build Cultural Architecture Around Care

- Systemise Wellbeing as Core Strategy.
  - » Don't add wellbeing on top. Integrate it into operations, planning cycles, KPIs and risk frameworks.
- Train Light-Sharing Leaders.
  - » Embed emotional agility, self-awareness, and energy stewardship into leadership development. Shift from command to connection.
- Map Market and Psychosocial Context.
  - » Align your culture work with ESG imperatives, ISO 45003 standards, and the mental health legislation that demands proactive responsibility.

Glow Lens: this is your application of Regenerative Leadership and Wellbeing-by-Design. It's how we make safety and care structural, not symbolic.

Profit Lens: embedding wellbeing improves ROI 4–6 times per dollar invested, reduces claims, and attracts values-aligned talent in a competitive market.

Phase 3: ACTIVATE
Move From Words to Rituals

- Launch a Behaviours Framework.
    » Translate your values into performance expectations. Make 'how we work' just as important as 'what we do'.
- Create Rhythmic Rituals.
    » Pulse and Reflect check-ins, Glowstorms, Wellbeing Circles – rituals are your cultural drumbeat.
- Develop Responsive Feedback Loops.
    » Build safety in dialogue. Make space for reflection, not reaction. Let feedback be fuel, not fear.

Glow Lens: this phase brings The Reflective Organisation to life. It reclaims time, honours voice, and restores agency.

Profit Lens: rituals and feedback systems improve innovation, reduce rework, and foster faster team integration and cohesion.

Phase 4: EVOLVE
Measure, Adapt and Glow Forward

- Track Cultural and Commercial Metrics Together.
    » Culture is not soft. It is a lead indicator of performance. Measure engagement, wellbeing, trust, innovation, and client satisfaction.

- Celebrate the Glow in Progress.
  » Don't just reward results. Recognise moments of courage, empathy, and shared light. Progress is the new perfection.
- Adapt Through Psychological Seasons.
  » Rest is not absence – it is optimisation. Calibrate your calendars around human cycles.

Glow Lens: this phase is the embodiment of Rhythmic Growth and Reflective Scaling. It teaches us to grow gently, deeply, and wisely.

Profit Lens: adaptive cultures outperform competitors by up to three times, reduce burnout costs, and increase sustainability across cycles.

Indicators of Commercial Glow

This roadmap delivers not just wellbeing, but wealth of a different kind. It transforms care into currency:

- up to 50 percent increase in productivity in psychologically safe teams
- 27 percent reduction in voluntary turnover (SecureTel case study)
- 16 percent revenue increase in one year following culture reset (mid-sized Facilities Management business)
- 41 percent reduction in turnover and 83 percent fewer sick days (Deloitte/WHO)
- 370 percent growth in innovation participation when fear is replaced with feedback

- 28,000 annual savings from one frontline idea in a re-cultured team
- up to $350,000 saved per prevented psychological injury claim
- $4 to $6 return per $1 invested in wellbeing programs.

A Culture That Pays Back

This is not about softening business. It is about strengthening it from the inside out.

When people feel seen, they rise. When leaders are grounded, they lead with less harm. When culture breathes, performance accelerates.

Glow is not a concept. It is your competitive edge.

Let this roadmap be your re-entry into the real work of leadership. Use the GLOW Toolkit and the embedded practices outlined throughout this book. You have the compass. Now take the step.

Start where you are.

Start small, but start fully. Build rhythm. Reflect often. Lead with light.

Glow forward.

To the Reader Who's Made It Here – You Are the Future

You didn't just read this book. You felt it.

And maybe, just maybe, it felt like home.

Because deep in you, there's always been a whisper that said, 'There must be another way.'

And now you know. There is.

You're not too late. You're not too soft. You're not too anything. You're ready.

This Is What Comes Next

- Start the conversation your workplace isn't ready for.
- Say what others only feel.
- Build the boardroom where glow is a strategy.
- Mentor the next leader who steers with heart, not just hustle.
- Redesign the policies, the posters, the review form, the site meeting – because you now know what's possible.

Phosphorescent intelligence was never mine to hold alone.

It was always meant to be passed on.

Now, it's yours to carry – into meetings, into moments, into the culture you're shaping.

Because one day, they'll look back and ask:

'How did we ever work any other way?'

And you'll answer – quietly, powerfully:

'We made a different choice. We chose to lead with light. We chose to glow.'

Acknowledgements

To every frontline worker, leader, cleaner, contractor, FM manager, and construction crew member who shared your stories—thank you. This book is grounded in your honesty and strength.

To the clients and organisations who chose to lead differently—you prove that change is not only possible but transformative.

To the Holistic Growth Solutions team: your dedication and heart inspire me daily. To Pinky, our very first team member—thank you for your loyalty and passion; you have been part of this journey from the very beginning.

To my family and friends—thank you for being my foundation. To my sisters, who embraced every part of me, including my neurodivergence, and to my brother, whose quiet leadership reflects our shared difference—I am deeply grateful.

To my parents, my lifelong cheerleaders—your belief in me has been my greatest fuel. To my partner, Mark—your steady presence and faith in this journey have meant more than words can hold.

To my mentors, who became friends, thank you for challenging me and opening doors so I could hold them open for others. To those who doubted the value of wellbeing—you sharpened my clarity and strengthened my conviction.

And to you, the reader—thank you for choosing to step into this work. You are the reason this glow continues to spread.

References

Foundational Psychology & Growth Mindset

Dweck, C. S. (2006). Mindset: The New Psychology of Success. Random House.

Seligman, M. E. P. (2011). Flourish: A Visionary New Understanding of Happiness and Wellbeing. Free Press. Duckworth, A. (2016). Grit: The Power of Passion and Perseverance. Scribner. Goleman, D. (1995). Emotional Intelligence: Why It Can Matter More Than IQ. Bantam Books.

Workplace Culture, Leadership & Inclusion

Brown, B. (2018). Dare to Lead: Brave Work. Tough Conversations. Whole Hearts. Random House.

Edmondson, A. (2019). The Fearless Organization: Creating Psychological Safety in the Workplace for Learning, Innovation, and Growth. Wiley.

Lencioni, P. (2002). The Five Dysfunctions of a Team: A Leadership Fable. Jossey-Bass.

Laloux, F. (2014). Reinventing Organizations: A Guide to Creating Organizations Inspired by the Next Stage of Human Consciousness.

Nelson Parker.

Wellbeing & Trauma-Informed Practice

WHO. (1998). Wellbeing Index (WHO-5).

van der Kolk, B. A. (2014). The Body Keeps the Score: Brain, Mind, and Body in the Healing of Trauma.

Viking.

Kabat-Zinn, J. (1994). Wherever You Go, There You Are: Mindfulness Meditation in Everyday Life.

Hyperion.

Organisational and ISO Frameworks

ISO 45003:2021 – Occupational health and safety management – Psychological health and safety at work – Guidelines for managing psychosocial risks.

ISO 45001:2018 – Occupational health and safety management systems – Requirements with guidance for use.

Google. (2015). Project Aristotle [Study on team effectiveness and psychological safety].

Business Case for Culture & Wellbeing

Deloitte. (2020). Mental health and employers: Refreshing the case for investment.

McKinsey & Company. (2021). Diversity Wins: How Inclusion Matters.

Harvard Business Review articles on culture, safety leadership, and trust as strategic assets (specific titles can be selected based on final citations used).

Self-Citations

Vallance, L. (2025). Phosphorescent Intelligence: Illuminating Growth, Holistic Wellbeing, and Resilient Culture in the Modern Workplace. Holistic Growth Solutions.

Holistic Growth Solutions. (2025). Phosphorescent Culture Diagnostic & Glow storming Tools [Unpublished internal framework].

Global Relevance Expansion

World Health Organization (WHO). (2010). Healthy workplace framework and model: Background and supporting literature and practices.

Geneva: World Health Organization. https://www.who.int/publications/i/ite m/9789241500241United Nations. (n.d.). Sustainable Development Goal 3: Good health and Wellbeing. United Nations Department of Economic and Social Affairs. https://sdgs.un.org/goals/goal3

United Nations. (n.d.). Sustainable Development Goal 8: Decent work and economic growth. United Nations Department of Economic and Social Affairs. https://sdgs.un.org/goals/goal8

www.ingramcontent.com/pod-product-compliance
Lightning Source LLC
Chambersburg PA
CBHW041305240426
43661CB00011B/1025